1   The organ-grinder – a familiar figure in yesterday's Dublin streets

2   (*overleaf*) Dubliners in a doorway in Ashe Street, off the Coombe

DUBLIN

from old photographs

Introduction and commentaries by

MAURICE GORHAM

B. T. BATSFORD LTD

LONDON

Text © Maurice Gorham 1972

First published 1972
Reprinted 1983

Printed by The Anchor Press Ltd, Tiptree, Essex
for the publishers B. T. Batsford Ltd
4 Fitzhardinge Street, London W1

ISBN 0 7134 0122 2

3   The Long Car was the only public transport out of Dublin until
the coming of the railway

CONTENTS

ACKNOWLEDGMENTS

Among those who have helped me, either by providing photographs or by giving information about them, my thanks are due to: The Abbey Theatre (Fig. 37); B. T. Batsford Ltd (6, 27, 28, 42–46); Douglas Bennett; Robert C. Booth and Michael E. Booth (119); Frank Burke (89, 90); Liam Byrne of the National Library of Ireland (8–16, 18–23, 29, 30, 32, 47–51, 53, 54, 57, 58, 60–62, 67, 68, 70, 71, 77, 121, 122, 135, 141); Dr H. S. Corran of the Guinness Museum (35, 39, 97, 98, 119, 123, 124, 144); Mrs Sidney Czira (95, 102, 113, 117, 118); Squadron-Leader H. Ellison (1, 25, 26, 56, 138, 146); Fr Sean Farraher, C.S.Sp. of Blackrock College (86, 88, 91, 93, 99, 100, 101, 105–108); Dr Patrick Flanagan; C. Flewitt (63); Major R. D. Greer of the Royal Irish Automobile Club (127, 128, 133); Patrick Healy (2, 7, 31, 57, 110, 112, 115, 148); A. V. Henry; Mrs William Jameson (Flora Mitchell) (72, 81, 109); Edmund Kelly (59); C. Gordon Lambert of Irish Biscuits Ltd (41); Robert Montgomery (69, 137); Fr John Moroney of Dun Laoghaire (52); Alan Newham; Rita O'Dea (116); Frank O'Reilly of Irish Distillers Group Ltd (120); Royal Dublin Society (4, 24, 82, 83); D. E. Stevens of Stevens Cycle Company (131, 132); Science Museum (40, 66); Knollys Stokes (130); Michael Tutty of the Old Dublin Society (3, 5, 33, 34, 38, 64, 65, 80, 84, 85, 94, 125, 134, 140, 147, 149, 150); Wanderers F. C. (87); Stella Webb (75, 111, 114, 126, 129); and Mairin Woods (46).

Also I owe a particular debt to F. E. Dixon (17, 73, 74, 76, 78, 79, 92, 96, 103, 139, 142, 143, 145), expert on old Dublin and collector of Victoriana, who has given me valuable assistance throughout.

4 Carlisle Bridge, Sackville Street, and Nelson's Pillar before the trams came in 1872 – much retouched, but a photograph beneath it all

INTRODUCTION

The camera came to Dublin in the early 'forties and found it in a state of flux; as indeed it had been ever since it first began to spread beyond the walls.

    The great age of building was over. The Wide Streets Commissioners had done their work; so had the Gardiners and Fitzwilliams and many another builder (they had not begun to call themselves 'developers' then). The wide streets were there, the great squares, and nearly all the great public buildings – Four Courts, Custom House, Bank of Ireland, King's Inns, and of course Trinity College. Even the railway had made its appearance: the line to Kingstown had opened in 1834.

The shape of the city had been fixed before photography began, with the main axis from St Stephen's Green to Rutland (now Parnell) Square by way of College Green and Carlisle (now, and for nearly a hundred years, O'Connell) Bridge. The old Parliament House had been the Bank of Ireland since the early years of the century; William III stood on his plinth outside it, despite periodical mutilations to horse and man; the General Post Office and Nelson's Pillar marked the climax of Sackville Street, with the Imperial and the Gresham hotels growing up around it as the century progressed.

The Castle was there all the time, of course, and the Viceregal Lodge in Phoenix Park, with all their pomp and circumstance – levees, drawing-rooms, Royal visits, and so on; and a constantly varying atmosphere, from that generated by a harsh Viceroy like Earl Spencer to that surrounding a liberal character like the Earl of Aberdeen, who brought the Viceroyalty closer to the people than it had ever been.

So the growth that the camera recorded, in the next 70 years, was growth of a different kind. Some public buildings, it is true: the group round Leinster House – the National Gallery and the small Museum in 1864, the National Library and the main Museum in 1890; the great railway stations, Broadstone, Kings-

5   Street scene – but what the chancer is selling to the photographers, nobody knows

bridge, Amiens Street, Harcourt Street. But most of what was built was more domestic. New hospitals, theatres, hotels; new statues in the streets, all of them – even O'Connell – subsidiary to the Pillar, that mistaken monument to Nelson; an occasional bridge across the Liffey, such as Butt Bridge and, at the end of the century, the great eyesore – the Loop Line Bridge, invaluable for carrying trains across the river, but wantonly, it seemed, brought round in front of the Custom House, as if it was intended to spoil the view. It is still there, though there is talk now of getting rid of it at last.

And of course there were the suburbs. Dublin was spreading fast. North and south of the river, but especially to the south, new houses, streets, churches and pubs were springing up, much helped by the spread of the railways and, later, the trams. What had been a compact city began to sprawl, out beyond the two circular roads which were meant to limit its growth, beyond the canals – everywhere but on the north-west, where the great spread of Phoenix Park blocked it off, and Castleknock remained a village for another 50 years.

What was changing all the time was the street scene, the look of people, what they wore, how they travelled, from the first horse-buses to the early motor-cars. (The motor-bus did not come to Dublin until long after 1910.) Even here everything did not change. The horse-trams gave way to electric, but these remained until well into modern times, surviving the growlers and sidecars that filled the streets 60 years ago.

But there were plenty of changes in the way people dressed, from the very tall top-hats of the men and the crinolines of the ladies in the 'forties and 'fifties through bustles and bowlers to the black pyramids of old ladies who still worshipped Queen Victoria and the fashionable frills of Edwardian times. And there were changes in the background – the shops and hotels. Not so many, though. Many of the shops are still there, many more have only recently been replaced by office blocks. As for the hotels, those in Sackville Street were destroyed in the troubles of 1916 to 1923, but the Shelbourne on Stephen's Green remains, to the outward eye, very much as it was when it was rebuilt in 1867. Only the canopy is new.

To me, at least, life looks very pleasant in most of these photographs. There were drawbacks, of course – muddy roads and a variety of smells (though we have no score nowadays to be superior about smells – the Liffey alone gives out smells that could not have been worse a hundred years ago); and there were dreadful slums. And besides the sheer grim poverty of many of the inhabitants there were constant political troubles that kept the police spies busy: O'Connell and Repeal, the Young Irelanders, the Fenians, the Invincibles, with the spectacular killing of Lord Frederick Cavendish and Mr T. H. Burke in Phoenix Park; Parnell and the Home Rule movement, Larkin and his strike, and finally – less easily discerned from Edwardian days – Connolly and Pearse and the men who were to go out in 1916.

But what the camera records is a general impression of uncrowded trams, with sidecars and horse-cabs always available, unhurried people walking freely among the traffic and stopping to talk in the middle of the road; a city on a human scale, with people not yet dwarfed by buildings (ugly though some of the buildings were). . . . It all has an atmosphere that arouses envy today.

There was a short film* shown recently in Dublin, in which photographs of nineteenth-century Dublin, from the Lawrence collection, were interspersed with moving pictures of Dublin today. It was a most effective film, but rather unfair to Lawrence's Dublin, or so it seemed to me. Lawrence photographs reproduced in monochrome against the brilliant colours of the present day (for present-day Dublin is usually photographed on days of brilliant sun), barefoot children in the street against well-dressed, well-shod children playing before a background of towering flats. . . . Even so, there was an air of tranquillity about the Lawrence Dublin as opposed to the rush and restlessness of today.

This Lawrence collection, housed in the National Library, which had the inspiration to buy it when Lawrence's business was sold up, is the most valuable source of photographs of late-Victorian and Edwardian Dublin, and indeed all Ireland. But it only began shortly before 1880, and it is very difficult to get good photographs from earlier than this. And of the 40,000 Lawrence plates that survive, all are landscapes or, often, streetscapes. His portraits, and any domestic subjects that his photographers took, were lost in 1916.

The task of collecting was made none the easier for me by the fact that Dublin had already been included in a collection that I made for Batsford a year or two ago.** Some very good Dublin photographs were in it, including one of Smith O'Brien and T. F. Meagher in Kilmainham Jail in 1849. I hope I have been able to find some new ones of equal interest for this book, though not many as early as 1849.

These photographs come from diverse sources, for except for the Lawrence collection, the work of Dublin photographers of the nineteenth century has mostly disappeared, or lapsed into private hands. There must be many more

*'Dubliners Sean agus Nua' ('Dubliners Old and New'), directed by Louis Marcus for Gael Linn.
**Ireland from Old Photographs, 1971

photographs lurking in people's boxrooms and attics – or, if few people now have boxrooms and attics, in old trunks under people's beds. Unfortunately many such collections have been thrown away, a fate that happens all too easily to old photographs in Ireland. Luckily a great many have survived, and glass negatives turn up now and again in auction-rooms, often without any knowledge as to who took them, and when and where.

Still, it can be said for these photographs that one can find in them not only reminders of the way our ancestors looked and dressed and travelled, and where they shopped, but reminders of many buildings that have been razed by the 'developers', as well as those that were destroyed in the years between 1916 and 1923, when the General Post Office was burnt out – the same fate that befell the Four Courts and the Custom House, in varying degrees. It is fortunate for us that these were all rebuilt on the old plans, unlike more recent casualties like the Carlisle Building at O'Connell Bridge, which went down before the 'developer' only a few years ago. It was replaced by one of Dublin's typical egg-boxes, eleven storeys high.

And there are a few samples of more intimate photographs, just to remind us of what families looked like 80 or 90 years ago.

6   Forgotten Dublin – the old mill on the last open stretch of the river Poddle, near St Patrick's Cathedral, about 1890. The river is now completely covered in

7 Market women – and children – in Patrick's Close

MAIN STEM

8 From St Stephen's Green by College Green to Rutland (now Parnell) Square has been Dublin's main thoroughfare ever since Carlisle Bridge was opened in 1791. Here is the start of the run – the North-West corner of Stephen's Green about 1875–80. In the latter year the park was opened to the public by Lord Ardilaun

9 Much the same scene 30 years later. The trams are now electric, there is a motor-car in the picture, and the triumphal arch has been erected to commemorate the deeds of the Dublin Fusiliers in the South African War. It was known to derisive Dubliners as the Traitors' Arch

10 The West side of Stephen's Green, with the College of Surgeons and a fine assortment of traffic – sidecar, carriages, trap, carts, and the horse-tram to Rathmines

11   Grafton Street, with the corner of Wicklow Street on the left and the façade of Trinity College at the foot

14   (*overleaf*) The William III statue in College Green, which was finally blown up in 1929, and the Guard leaving the Bar

12   The bottom of Grafton Street, with the East front of the Bank of Ireland in the distance – and a sidecar proceeding placidly on the wrong side of the road. Barnardo's, the furriers, is still there, and North, estate agents, only recently moved

13   The Bank of Ireland on College Green, with two types of horse-tram and Grattan's statue, which is still there

15　Westmoreland Street, leading down to the bridge, with Tom Moore's statue on the right

17 Eden Quay from Bachelor's Walk – an early photograph showing one of Dublin's short-lived horse-buses crossing Carlisle Bridge, the masts of shipping that then came right up to the bridge, and, in the foreground, a gentleman looking rather incongruous in his shirt-sleeves

(*opposite*) O'Connell Bridge (the name was changed from Carlisle in 1880, when bridge was widened), with the statue of William Smith O'Brien in the foreground the O'Connell Monument towering on the far side. The horse-trams have knife-d seats on top

18 Sackville Street, the General Post Office, and the Pillar. The Post Office was burnt out in 1916 but restored, the Pillar was blown up in 1966. The statue is of Sir John Gray, who got Dublin its water supply, the Vartry scheme

19 A later photograph of the same view – about 1891 – with O'Connell Bridge, Butt Bridge, and the hideous Loop Line Bridge that still takes the railway across the river

20 (*opposite*) Flower-sellers at the Pillar – and a glimpse of Earl Street

21   The top of Sackville Street about 1902 – with the original Gresham Hotel

22   The end of the run – the Parnell Memorial and the beginning of Rutland Square; the Rotunda Hospital is on the left. This is a late picture. The Rotunda Assembly Room did not become a cinema until 1910 – and there is a covered-top tram

ROUND THE TOWN

23　At the top of Earlsfort Terrace: in the background, the Exhibition Palace, built for the Exhibition of 1865, extended for the Royal University of Ireland (1882 to 1908–9). It was replaced by a new building for the National University

25 Amiens Street station, built 1844–46, the great age of station-building in Dublin. It is still there – though it is now called Connolly Station, after the 1916 leader – and it still carries trains to the North

pposite) Workmen on the job of building the theatre in Leinster House, then occupied by yal Dublin Society. It now serves as the meeting-place of Dail Eireann

26 The Mater – the famous North-side hospital, built in 1860. Its full title is the Mater Misericordiae Hospital

27, 28 Two scenes in old Dublin – Weaver's Square and Brown Street, both even then looking much the worse for wear

29 Leinster Market, behind D'Olier Street – and a few of its inhabitants

30 A typical nineteenth-century Dublin slum – Poole Street, with the washing hanging out. What a heroic job it was to do the washing, too, in this sort of street

31 In Chamber Street, round the corner from Weaver's Square. The gabled houses are typical of this neighbourhood

32   St Michael's Lane, off High Street, just behind Christ Church cathedral

33 A revivalist preaching in the street, with a discreet escort of police

34 (*overleaf*) Whipping-tops in Bride Street – and, apparently, no worries about traffic

35 Up-river – Guinness loading their famous steam barges at Victoria Quay, about 1904

36 Strange as it seems, it is very hard to find photographs of the original Abbey Theatre, which was burnt down in 1951. This photograph shows the theatre as it originally was, with the gabled canopy that was later replaced by a semi-circular one; but it was not taken until 1913

37 A scene from a typical Abbey production of 1910 – *Birthright*, by T. C. Murray

38 Open-air market – delf on display in unpromising surroundings

39 Part of Guinness's brewery, about 1895: the foot of Steevens's Lane, with the railway line running to Kingsbridge Station (just out of the picture, bottom right). The Nurses' Home opposite is still there

40 The Black Church, built by John Semple in 1830, was photographed about 1843 by William Henry Fox Talbot, the pioneer of photography. It is still there, though no longer used as a church

41 Peter Row in 1896, when Jacobs had just opened their new factory, from which they are now moving out. Prominent among the posters are two for *Charley's Aunt*

42 The Four Courts, seen from across the Liffey. Gandon's splendid building of 1786–1802 was badly damaged in 1922, when the dome was destroyed, but it has been restored

43   Leinster House, the East front, looking on to Merrion Square. The statue to Prince Albert was moved across to the side of the Museum when the obelisk to the founders of the State was raised

44   The Bedford Tower over the Office of Arms in the Castle – now the Genealogical Office and Heraldic Museum – with a couple of the garrison posing by the lamp-post

45 The City Hall, built by
Thomas Cooley – 1769 to
1779 – as the Royal
Exchange

46 The College of
Surgeons on St Stephen's
Green

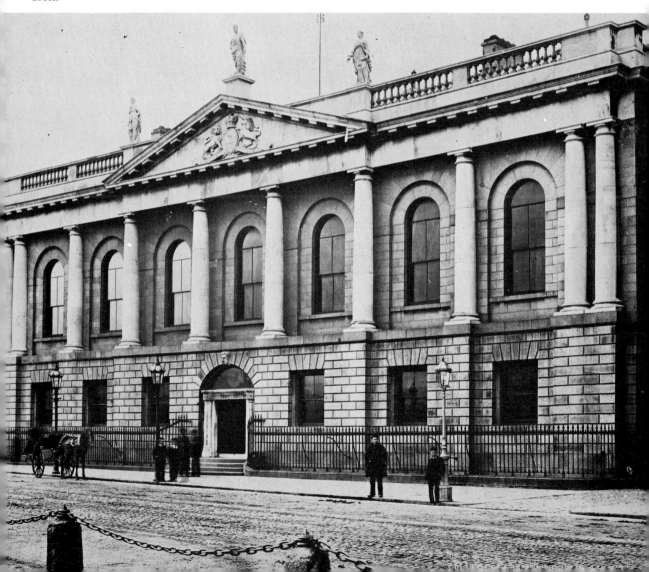

47 (*previous page*) The view up the river from Gandon's great Custom House. On the right is Custom House Quay, followed by Eden Quay and Bachelor's Walk (beyond the bridge); on the left, old Butt Bridge (the swing-bridge built in 1879) and Burgh Quay across the river

48 The view down the Liffey towards the sea, with the Custom House facing a litter of merchandise and a paddle steamer

SUBURBS AND OUTSKIRTS

49   The Victoria Memorial at Kingstown – now Dun Laoghaire – with the mailboat beyond

50 The East Pier at Kingstown has always been a popular resort for people in search of fresh air, a view, and a band. The paddle-steamer seems to be the R.M.S. *Ireland*, which was launched in 1885, when she was the fastest merchant ship afloat

51 Another popular resort – the Pavilion at Kingstown, now gone; two waitresses standing in the doorway as if they have spotted the photographer

52 A busy scene in George's Street, Kingstown, in the early years of the century, with the Dalkey tram on its way

53 Holiday atmosphere on Killiney Strand, with the military well to the fore

54 (*opposite*) A distant view of the strand, with teas, tents, a lot of people paddling, and a few actually bathing

55, 56, 57 The Hill of Howth, on the other side of Dublin, was another great place for holidays. On the left, children of 1896 gather round a street harper; above, a picnic on the Summit; and below, the Hill of Howth tram arrives at the Summit. This tram outlived all the others in Dublin by ten years – Coras Iompair Eireann did not kill it until 1959

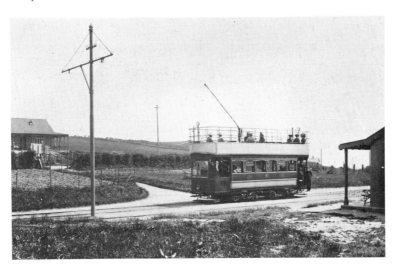

58 Baggot Street Bridge on the Grand Canal – Herbert Place and Haddington Road beyond, with St Mary's church and Baggot Street Hospital in the distance. This photograph was taken in the early 1900s, but except for the right-hand bank of the canal, the scene is unchanged today

59   The beach at Bray, with Bray Head beyond

60   The park at Blackrock

61 On the river at Islandbridge on Boat Race Day

62 A very small procession leaves Phoenix Park by Parkgate – presumably coming from the Viceregal Lodge

63 The Western gate at Kilmainham, with its Highland guard. This gate, designed by Francis Johnston, originally stood on the quays, but when Kingsbridge station was built the Great Southern and Western Railway moved it – at their own expense

64 Visiting the Strawberry Beds. This pleasant spot, on the North bank of the Liffey, was a favourite resort of Dubliners having a day out

65 The ass-cart is tethered outside the Post Office at Kilmacanogue, Co. Wicklow, just under the
Sugar Loaf, Dublin's own particular mountain

66 And here is a Fox Talbot photograph of Powerscourt, Co. Wicklow, taken about 1843

67   The Viceregal Lodge in Phoenix Park, abode of Viceroys since 1816, now the residence of the President of Ireland

68   The steam tram from Dublin at the Spa Hotel, Lucan, Co. Dublin

69   A domestic scene in Terenure, about 1900

70 Rathmines Road in the days of four-wheelers and sidecars. Findlaters shops were a great feature of Dublin until very recent times.

71 The end of the line: the Sandymount tram at the Martello Tower. The tower now contains a shop, and another shop is built on to it, but except for the tramlines, Strand Road beyond is unchanged

PEOPLE

72 Crew party in Kingstown: the crew of Sir Thomas Lipton's steam yacht *Erin* pose for a spoof photograph in 1901. The *Erin* went to the United States with Lipton's *Shamrock II*, and some of the men in the photograph crewed *Shamrock* for her three races for the America's Cup

74 All aboard for the water-chute at the great Dublin Exhibition of 1907: adults very happy and the children looking a shade nervous

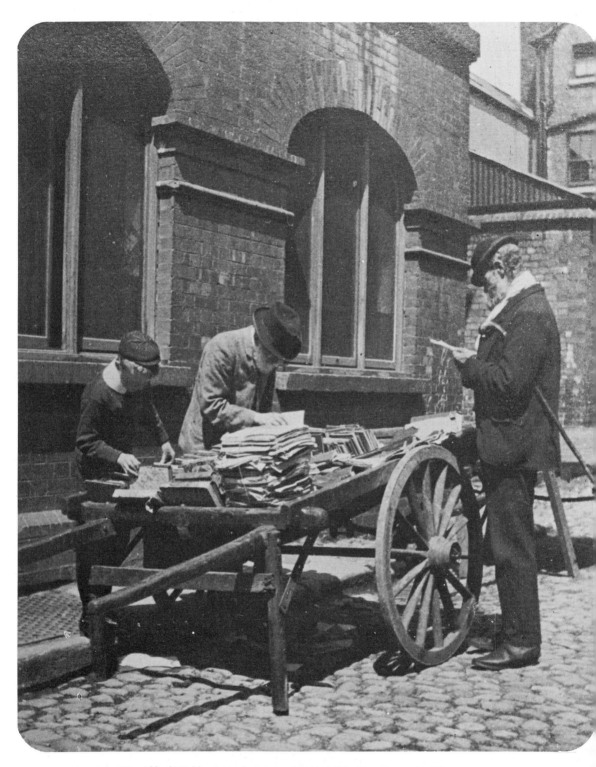

75 Alfred Webb snapped at a street bookstall in Fleet Street, Dublin

76 'Irish Street Merchant Having a Quiet Smoke' is the caption to this Victorian post-card (printed in Germany)

77 The grave of Charles Stewart Parnell, the Irish leader, in Glasnevin cemetery, in 1891, the year that he died

78 An afternoon on the terrace of the 1907 Exhibition   **79** (*below*) Down the water-chute at the Exhibition

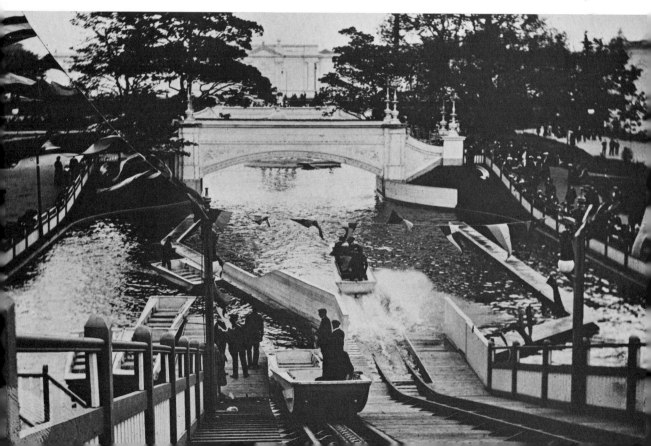

80   The great Edwardian seaside sport – paddling

81 A gay scene at Malahide Flower Show

82 · And another at the Dublin Horse Show in 1908

83 Winnie II, winner of the first prize in Class 16 at the RDS Spring Show of 1899. Her owner and breeder, Thomas Boylan of Drogheda, is with her, and his son, later Brigadier E. T. Boylan, holds her halter. He in turn was the father of Major Eddie Boylan, well known in show-jumping circles today

84 Lansdowne v. Bective in the Leinster Cup of 1891. Note the long shorts – well below the knee

85　A street cobbler plies his trade

87 (*right*) Sport in the 'eighties – Wanderers' knicker-bocker Rugby XV of 1887–8. Captain, G. Stoker

86 And in the 'sixties – boys of the French College demonstrating boxing, fencing, archery, handball, and every form of gymnastics, in 1866. The French College later became known as Blackrock

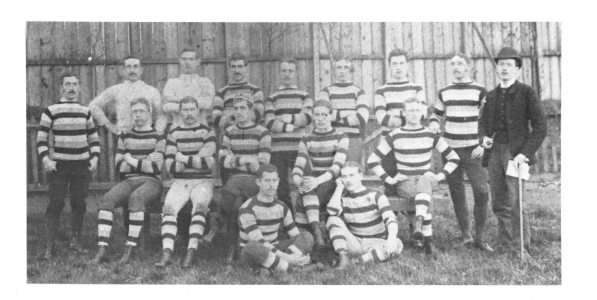

88 Here is a cricket team from the French College in 1866 – the little boys wearing their uniform trousers, with a broad stripe

Sgoil Éanna, Rát Feaṗnáin : Peileaḋóiṗí (Sóiṗiṗ), Luċt ḃuaiḋṫe Cuṗaḋ-ṁíṗ Baile Áṫa Cliaṫ, 1910-11.
St. Enda's College, Rathfarnham : Junior Football Team, Holders of Dublin Schools Cup, 1910-11.
P. Ḃṗeaṫnaċ, R. Macaṁlaoiḃ, Ḃ. Ó Tuaṫail, S. MacDiaṗmaḋa, S. Ó Dúnlaing, P. Ó Maolṁuaiḋ, C. Mac Fionnlaoiċ
F. Ó Doċaṗtaiġ, S. Ó Duḃġaill, Ḃ. Seoiġe, F. de Búṗca (Taoiṗeaċ), U. Ó Cúlaċáin, Ḃ. Ó Cléiṗiġ,
C. Ó Cléiṗiġ, S. Ó Conċoḃaiṗ.

89, 90 The junior football team of St Enda's, Padraig Pearse's famous school, in 1910–11, captain Frank Burke, and the junior hurling team of the same year, captain Sean MacDermot. Both teams were winners of that year's Dublin Schools Cup. It was Frank Burke who ran the school when it was revived, after Pearse's death, in 1920

Sgoil Éanna, Rát Feaṗnáin : Iománaiḋṫe (Sóiṗiṗ), Luċt ḃuaiḋṫe Cuṗaḋ-ṁíṗ Baile Áṫa Cliaṫ, 1910-11.
St. Enda's College, Rathfarnham : Junior Hurling Team, Holders of Dublin Schools Cup, 1910-11.
S. Ó Conċoḃaiṗ, P. Ḃṗeaṫnaċ, R. Mac Aṁlaoiḃ, Ḃ. Ó Tuaṫail, S. Ó Duḃġaill, S. Ó Dúnlaing, E. MacDaiḃeaċ,
C. Mac Fionnlaoiċ, U. Ó Cúlaċáin, S. Mac Diaṗmaḋa (Taoiṗeaċ), Ḃ. Seoiġe, U. Ó Tuaṫail, T. Ó hOiṗín,
S. Ó hOiṗín, S. Paoṗ.

91   The French College First XI of 1882–3 – when cricketers could dress more picturesquely that they can today

92   When the Australians played Dublin University Past and Present, in June 1905, this was the Dublin team. Captain, F. H. Browning

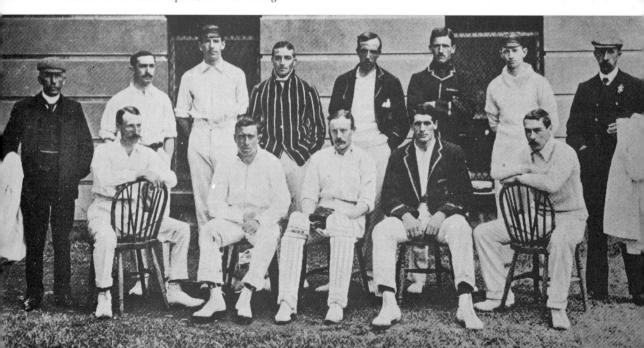

93   The Rugby team of 1882, from the Civil Service side of Blackrock

95 A Markievicz production of *The Devil's Disciple* at the Gaiety in 1913. Madame Markievicz and the Count are sitting in the middle (with Madame's dog) with Breffni O'Rourke on his right. Sidney Gifford, later known as John Brennan, is behind Madame, with Helena Moloney on her right and Michael Noyek on her left. The soldiers were drawn from the Count's friends, the rebels from Madame's

96 'The Old Style' – these four constituted the nursing staff of the Meath Hospital a hundred years ago

MEATH HOSPITAL NURSES, 20 YEARS AGO, 1872.

| FEVER NURSE | NIGHT NURSE | SURGICAL NURSE | ACCIDENT NURSE |
| HODGENS. | SPRING. | MURRAY. | BRAZIL. |

97 (*previous page*) The gallopers at the Guinness show at Ballsbridge, and **98** (*above*) the special trams that brought people back from the show; about 1900–1904

99 University students of 1882: students for degrees of the Royal University of Ireland in front of Williamstown Castle. Note the man in the mortar-board, standing against the tree

100 The workmen employed on the demolition of Williamstown Avenue, to enlarge Blackrock College, in 1904–5. With them are the lodge-keeper's wife and the brother in charge of the work, Brother Mary Paul

CLOSE UP

101 Blackrock uniform in 1866: this was the dress
worn by pupils of the Holy Ghost fathers when they
came to Williamstown from France in 1860

102 The Pearse brothers, Willie (*left*) and Padraig – a rare photograph of the two who were shot in 1916

103 An early photographic book illustration: Archdeacon Henry Irwin, Archdeacon of Emly· and Chaplain of Sandford, Dublin: from his 'Remains' by the Rev. W. Pakenham Walsh, A.M., published in 1858

104 A Lafayette study of Kate Kelly, about 1885, who later became an ardent Suffragette; she was sent to jail in England for lying hidden all night on the canopy of Westminster Horticultural Hall and pouring a pail of whitewash over Lloyd George. She worked for Irish prisoners in England during and after the first World War

105, 106 Youth of a President: Eamon de Valera (bareheaded) as a boy in class at Blackrock in 1898 and (above, in the bowler) as a young man at the Golden Jubilee celebrations in 1911. Beyond him, in the top hat, is Richard Kelly, owner of the *Tuam Herald*

107 And here is the young de Valera (*far left*) in a school cycle race in 1903. His starter is James A. Sweeney, a famous athlete and Rugby international

108 Patrick J. Kelly's high jump of 1888. The record that he made with this jump stood for many years

109 Engaged! Arthur J. C. Mitchell and Margaret Norman, in 1887

110 Charles Russell, the artist, and his family at domestic croquet, also in 1887

GOLDEN WEDDING OF THOMAS AND MARY WEBB 1883

Lizzie Webb
daughter of Thos & Mary

Arthur Webb
son of Thos & Mary

Emilie Margaret Webb
(née Watson) wife of Arthur

Thomas Henry Webb
son of Thos & Mary

Emily Webb
daughter of Thos & Mary

Josephine Webb
daughter of Thos & Mary

Emily Webb
(née Charles) wife of
Thos. Hy.

THOMAS WEBB

Anna Marion Webb
daughter of Arthur

Grace Webb
daughter of Thos Hy.

MARY WEBB
(née Fisher)

Charlotte Webb
daughter of Thos & Mary

Leonard Webb

Roger Webb

111 A Golden Wedding of 1883: Thomas and Mary Webb (née Fisher) on the great occasion, with their sons and daughters, a couple of daughters-in-law and grandchildren – everybody in the picture was called Webb

112 Charles Russell with his art class. Seated in the middle is believed to be Estella Solomons, the distinguished etcher who married the poet Seumas O'Sullivan (Dr Starkey), founder and editor of the *Dublin Magazine*

113 Three rebels – Tom Clarke (standing) with John Daly (*left*) and Sean MacDermot, photographed in 1911. Clarke and MacDermot were shot in 1916

114 Two Quaker ladies – Susanna Watson (née Davis) and her daughter Anna Bewley, in the garden at Sandford Grove

115 'The Cottage' at Irishtown, in front of which the Beatty family were photographed in 1872 – a charming reminder of what a seaside village Irishtown used to be

116   Mrs Martha O'Dea with her three boys, about 1901. Ken, the baby on her knee, became a pianist. Lawrence, on the right, became well known as Lionel Day of the Radio Eireann Repertory Players, and as the President of the Old Dublin Society. Jimmy, in the middle, already at 18 months has the face of the great comedian that he was to become.

117, 118 Countess
Markievicz; and, below,
herself as Suffrage rescuing
Kathleen Houston
(Professor Houston's
daughter) in one of the
tableaux that she used to get
up. Her armour was home-
made – from lino

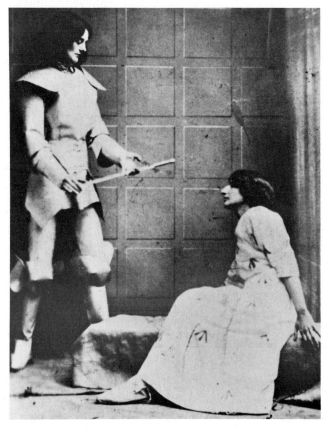

GETTING ABOUT

119 William Booth leads the way on a bicycle made for two, with 'Min' McKell, in 1901 or 1902

120 Four-in-hands of the 1890s outside the Shelbourne Hotel. From left to right – Mr Thompson, Mr Waterhouse, Mr Joseph O'Reilly, himself driving. The O'Reilly greys are Infidel, Triumph, Killarney and Killorglin. The Shelbourne is as it is now, except that there is no canopy outside the front door

121 (*left*) A couple of sidecars by the Wellington Testimonial in Phoenix Park; and
122 (*right*) a show specimen – car, horse and driver

123, 124 Guinness transport: above, a prize-winning dray and below, the first steam vehicle that they owned, with its crew, in 1900

125 Contrast in styles: cyclists out from Dublin encounter a slide cart

126 Family party: the Bewley family, with two of the men mounted on penny-farthing tricycles

127 Major Guillamore O'Grady, a well-known figure around the turn of the century, at the wheel of his 1898–9 Daimler, with his valet in the tonneau

128 The fourth Gordon Bennett race was held in Ireland in 1903, with speed trials in Phoenix Park (see James Joyce's short story 'After the Race' in *Dubliners*). Here is the winner, Janetzy, a Belgian, known as the Red Devil from his bushy beard, driving a 4-cylinder Mercedes for Germany; followed by the whole French team. His average speed was 49·2 m.p.h., though he did 80–90 on the straight

129 Here is the Gordon Bennett course, on the Curragh; Janetzy in the middle distance

130 Setting out for a rally from the garage of the Royal Irish Automobile Club about 1906. The garage, in Dawson Street, has now been converted to house the premises of the Club

131 Cycling champion of 1900 – Jack Mead, of the National Cycling Club

132 Motor-cycling champion: R. W. Stevens, photographed on 15 October 1902. He was winner of the first scratch race in Ireland, first hill-climbing competition, first reliability speed trial – and maker of the Phoenix, the first motor-cycle made in Ireland

133 Early motor-cars photographed in the garage of the Royal Irish Automobile Club: all the cars in the picture were made before 1905

135 Kingstown Harbour crowded for the Regatta; and a little family party, down on the sward

134 (*previous page*) This is a mystery picture. Anybody can see that it shows nine gentlemen seated on a monster five-wheeled penny-farthing, but who they were, what they were, and how they ever got round corners, nobody has revealed – so far

136 A couple of craft in Kingstown harbour, with H.M.S. *Melampus* beyond

137 When the mails went by paddle steamer – the City of Dublin Company's R.M.S. *Ulster* (built 1860), leaving Kingstown pier

138 The royal yacht in Kingstown Harbour, with the guardship H.M.S. *Melampus* in the background again. The black flags that she appears to be flying must be a trick of the camera – no reason for them is known

POMP

139 King Edward VII and Queen Alexandra visited Dublin for the 1907 Exhibition in what is now Herbert Park. Here they are, sharing the carriage with the Viceroy, the Marquess, and the Marchioness of Aberdeen

141   Sackville Street decorated for a royal visit. The Dublin Bread Company headquarters, with its extraordinary top-hamper, was one of Dublin's shortest-lived buildings. It was begun in 1901 and largely destroyed in 1916

140   (*previous page*) Two ordinary Dubliners come away from the Castle while the carriage and the escort wait for somebody important to come out. Note the condition of the roadway

142 The Aberdeens *en famille*. The Marquess came to Ireland as Viceroy in 1886, when this photograph was taken, but he is best remembered for his second Viceroyalty, from 1905 to 1915

143 The opening of the Children's Pavilion at Peamount: H. H. Asquith, the United Kingdom statesman, between the children, the Aberdeens at the foot of the steps

144 Crowds gathered for Queen Victoria's last visit, in 1900, watch a Guinness barge go by. The barge is gaily decorated, but it has the usual cargo – porter and stout

145 King George V and Queen Mary also came to Dublin, on a Coronation visit, in 1911

146 An intimate glimpse of the Aberdeens in their carriage, with a guest, in what looks rather like Pembroke Road

147 A couple of officers arriving in the Castle – to the surprise of the little dog.

148 A very small procession goes down one side of Sackville Street. On the far side is the old Hotel Metropole, later replaced by the Metropole Cinema, now to be demolished in its turn

149 A scene in the Upper Yard of the Castle on a levee day in the '90s; the two ladies seem to be rather in the way

150 Correctly dressed for the levee – but not thought much of by the three young Dubliners on the right